Christmas Tree

Ten Poems of Wishes and Lights

Candlestick Press

Published by:
Candlestick Press,
Diversity House, 72 Nottingham Road, Arnold, Nottingham NG5 6LF, UK
www.candlestickpress.co.uk

Design and typesetting by Craig Twigg

Printed by Bayliss Printing Company Ltd of Worksop, UK

Selection and Introduction © Di Slaney, 2025

Cover illustration © Sara Boccaccini Meadows, 2025
https://www.boccaccinimeadows.com

Candlestick Press monogram © Barbara Shaw, 2008

© Candlestick Press, 2025

ISBN 978 1 913627 58 4

Acknowledgements

The poems in this pamphlet are reprinted from the following books, all by
permission of the publishers listed unless stated otherwise. Every effort has been
made to trace the copyright holders of the poems published in this book. The
editor and publisher apologise if any material has been included without
permission, or without the appropriate acknowledgement, and would be glad to
be told of anyone who has not been consulted.

Thanks are due to all the copyright holders cited below for their kind permission.

Sinéad Morrissey, poem commissioned by The Poetry Society in 2021, by kind
permission of the author. https://poetrysociety.org.uk/

Thanks are also due to the authors below for their kind permission to use their
poems, all of which are published here for the first time:

Jeanette Burton, Olga Dermott-Bond, Gail Lawler, CP Nield, Rhona Stephens,
Molly Thapviwat and Polly Walshe.

All permissions cleared courtesy of Dr Suzanne Fairless-Aitken
c/o Swift Permissions swiftpermissions@gmail.com.

Where poets are no longer living, their dates are given.

Contents   Page

Introduction

Decorating a Christmas tree can bring great comfort as we untangle the fairy lights, hang up our baubles and tinsel, and rediscover treasures from our childhood or gifts from friends. It's a ritual many of us look forward to each year, whether we leave it till the last minute (guilty!) or start planning this year's festive colourway in October in line with the latest trends.

The Christmas tree poems in this special anthology are a mix of old and new, as the best traditions always are. We have seven new poems by contemporary poets who look at different ways of celebrating the tree, including CP Nield building a "tree of all the trees" made entirely of books (the poem displays in two different ways), and Olga Dermott-Bond's lyric retelling of a Ukrainian folk tale about a spider spinning webs as silken decorations.

Rhona Stephens' poignant poem takes us on a winter walk with father and son to choose their tree, while Molly Thapviwat perfectly captures the "ritual of dust and remembering" in bringing out the tree each year. Of course, no Christmas selection should be without some frost and here we have Robert Frost's magnificently chatty and confiding circular letter to a friend, where we learn the potential value of a plantation of Christmas trees and the art of negotiation.

We open this anthology with ee cummings' lovely poem about a little tree where spangles are "dreaming of being taken out and allowed to shine". I'm delighted to bring these ten wonderful Christmas tree poems to you to have their chance to shine, and hope that you'll love them as much as I do.

Di Slaney

[little tree]

little tree
little silent Christmas tree
you are so little
you are more like a flower

who found you in the green forest
and were you very sorry to come away?
see   i will comfort you
because you smell so sweetly

i will kiss your cool bark
and hug you safe and tight
just as your mother would,
only don't be afraid

look   the spangles
that sleep all the year in a dark box
dreaming of being taken out and allowed to shine,
the balls the chains red and gold the fluffy threads,

put up your little arms
and i'll give them all to you to hold
every finger shall have its ring
and there won't be a single place dark or unhappy

then when you're quite dressed
you'll stand in the window for everyone to see
and how they'll stare!
oh but you'll be very proud

and my little sister and i will take hands
and looking up at our beautiful tree
we'll dance and sing
"Noel Noel"

ee cummings (1894 – 1962)

Our Book Tree (i)

We build our Christmas tree each year,
pulling down books
from every shelf,
piling them up and up
on the living-room floor,

and planting the books,
we sniff the pages,
share sweet silver syllables,
words that bring us joy
from distant skies, from dreaming forests,

and soon a mound of books becomes
a mountain, a pyramid,
one miraculous pine
tottering, tapering
to tickle the ceiling,

a shrine tree wound in lights, a spine tree,
a hundred spines, a thousand, more,
a golden bough
with roots of books, leaves of books,
buds, blossoms, blazes of books,

a gift from the dying and the dead
for us, dear readers,
our tree of knowledge, our great ash tree,
our tree of all the trees,
our Christmas tree,

and perched on top,
a shy, tattered, coffee-stained paperback star.

CP Nield

Our Book Tree (ii)

Start from the last line and read up

.

star
paperback
coffee-stained
a shy, tattered,
and perched on top,
our Christmas tree,
our tree of all the trees,
our great ash tree,
our tree of knowledge,
for us, dear readers,
from the dying and the dead
blazes of books, a gift
leaves of books, buds, blossoms,
a golden bough with roots of books,
a hundred spines, a thousand, more,
a shrine tree wound in lights, a spine tree,
tottering, tapering to tickle the ceiling,
a mountain, a pyramid, one miraculous pine
forests, and soon a mound of books becomes
that bring us joy from distant skies, from dreaming
the books, we sniff the pages, share sweet silver syllables, words
shelf, piling them up and up on the living-room floor, and planting
We build our Christmas tree each year, pulling down books from every

CP Nield

Christmas Trees

A Christmas Circular Letter

The city had withdrawn into itself
And left at last the country to the country;
When between whirls of snow not come to lie
And whirls of foliage not yet laid, there drove
A stranger to our yard, who looked the city,
Yet did in country fashion in that there
He sat and waited till he drew us out
A-buttoning coats to ask him who he was.
He proved to be the city come again
To look for something it had left behind
And could not do without and keep its Christmas.
He asked if I would sell my Christmas trees;
My woods—the young fir balsams like a place
Where houses all are churches and have spires.
I hadn't thought of them as Christmas Trees.
I doubt if I was tempted for a moment
To sell them off their feet to go in cars
And leave the slope behind the house all bare,
Where the sun shines now no warmer than the moon.
I'd hate to have them know it if I was.
Yet more I'd hate to hold my trees except
As others hold theirs or refuse for them,
Beyond the time of profitable growth,
The trial by market everything must come to.
I dallied so much with the thought of selling.
Then whether from mistaken courtesy
And fear of seeming short of speech, or whether
From hope of hearing good of what was mine,
I said, 'There aren't enough to be worth while.'

'I could soon tell how many they would cut,
You let me look them over.'

                                    'You could look.
But don't expect I'm going to let you have them.'
Pasture they spring in, some in clumps too close

That lop each other of boughs, but not a few
Quite solitary and having equal boughs
All round and round. The latter he nodded 'Yes' to,
Or paused to say beneath some lovelier one,
With a buyer's moderation, 'That would do.'
I thought so too, but wasn't there to say so.
We climbed the pasture on the south, crossed over,
And came down on the north.

He said, 'A thousand.'

'A thousand Christmas trees!—at what apiece?'

He felt some need of softening that to me:
'A thousand trees would come to thirty dollars.'

Then I was certain I had never meant
To let him have them. Never show surprise!
But thirty dollars seemed so small beside
The extent of pasture I should strip, three cents
(For that was all they figured out apiece),
Three cents so small beside the dollar friends
I should be writing to within the hour
Would pay in cities for good trees like those,
Regular vestry trees whole Sunday Schools
Could hang enough on to pick off enough.
A thousand Christmas trees I didn't know I had!
Worth three cents more to give away than sell
As may be shown by a simple calculation.
Too bad I couldn't lay one in a letter.
I can't help wishing I could send you one
In wishing you herewith a Merry Christmas.

Robert Frost (1874 - 1963)

Just Keep Walking

Shut the gate behind you. And I do,
then stride the bramble-bordered gravel lane
until I reach the road. A left turn south.
Watch out for traffic coming. And I do.
Then left again along the puddle-walk until
two roads diverge. *We'll take the right*, Dad says.
And so I do - along the one I tripped on years ago,
a fisted stone ambushing me, but *I'll be fine*, I said.
That's right, said Dad. *That's right, lad,*
just keep walking. And I do.
A sharp left turn past Ewan King's,
his lollop of a dog all sniff and slather.
Carry on, lad, just keep walking. And I do,
along the grassy path, by birch and beech
to where the lean larch, sparse and golden,
lights December. Down the dip-path to
the bouncing tree, lain horizontal over granite rocks.
Don't slip. Stay close behind me. And I do,
a side-step into line, a shadow to his substance,
grass replaced by quiet moss beneath
my winter feet. The salad bowl, we call it, rising
steeply from its hollow to the rim where
it becomes a single track straight road.
Make sure to listen out for lorries. And I do,
for this is forestry commission land.
Right turn by arrow point until we reach
the timber yard and choose our tree.
Come on, lad, lend a hand here. And I do,
angling that year's conifer so Dad
can hoist it to his shoulders.
Some day soon, he said last year,
it will be you who'll carry home the tree.
Remember, lad, to set a steady pace,
then just keep walking. And I do.

Rhona Stephens

The Fourth King

They found me high
above the breathing canopy,
tightjacketed prodigy—
interstellar silence
laced through my hair
and frost like a tapestry
nailed to my door.

Such absolute dark
above my tippy-top
spangled crown,
ballooning sky-shot
Arctic greens draped
winter's finest shawl
about my shoulders.

Unstable starship
of the planet,
your lungs are my fingers—
their feather-thin million
branching endings:
tiny-bright tiny-light
redeemers of air.

Spectacular child
in the barn, who fell
like a comet or windfall,
I also attend—
I also stand, in all
my pine-needle finery,
and shine.

Sinéad Morrissey

Needled

Con
-ifers do
much prefer
not to live in. When you
hear them chat it sounds unflattering.
We are movers, they say, *not standers. We are not
stiff arrangements – that's all about you –
and – note this – we give feedback. We'd like to scrap
your gatherings. Your jumpers. Often we laugh.
You think it's the baubles tinkling.
Think again. Think on.*
Their fears: a roaring hearth, a limb
shorn off, bald areas.
Their least favourite word is
snap.
The trees are dry in their humour.
Green wood into dry,
they say, referring loosely to the Scriptures.
Oh yes, they are learned. And linguists. Their memory's
unparalleled. In fact they hate parallels, and all clean angles.
Right angles, they say, *we hate surtout.*
They remember what happened when their flesh
was chopped and set up crosswise.
After that they only wanted to be left alone
to wave their arms about.

They've been waving about
a long time. *Waving, not
drowning*, they stress,
being well-read.

Polly Walshe

Gown of Needles

In the hush before visitors
I unzip the tree from its net –
needles flick like green pins,
perfumed with frost and forest tales.
It stands, stiff-limbed and proud,
shoulders braced against the long
dark nights.

Here is my mother, hung in memory,
passing me a plush angel to perch
at the top. She says hush, hush now,
listen for old carols in the boughs.
I whisper the lines, half-lost in
cinnamon dreams and stories of reindeer
that slip through slanted moonlight.

Golden baubles catch my reflection
in miniature: a child's wide eyes,
a quickening of breath. Outside,
the sky is a black-lace veil, studded
with flickering spark. Inside, the tree
claims its space, cloaked in glitter,
wearing winter's hush like a crown.

Later, after all the gifts have unwrapped
themselves into laughter, I sense
the pine breathe in my quiet home –
small comfort, alive with a slow, green pulse.
January will come, gather up the hours,
but for now, each needle is a promise,
each branch a lullaby of light.

Gail Lawler

The Owl in the Christmas Tree

must have thought it a strange forest floor,
this living room with its tufts of sofa,

sprouting TV, grandfather clock, fireplace,
lamp-saplings, oak dresser budding trinkets,

four-legged beasts dozy with watchful waiting.
Overhead, a white sky, canopy of garlands,

no rain, but warm, reminiscent of the egg.
And light, so much light, blossoming

candied oranges, berries, pinecones, an angel.
And when the owl returned to the woods,

there must have been times at twilight hunt
when she hooted for those lost little gods,

the ones who kindled the sun at daybreak,
who conjured the darkness at nightfall.

Jeanette Burton

'A family in Kentucky had a surprise when a small owl was discovered nestled
in their Christmas tree – the bird had gone unnoticed for several days.'
BBC News, December 2023.

Once Upon a Christmas Eve

a poor widow and her children slept
while a spider cast her spell, spinning
webs downstairs, moon after perfect moon

across their little fir tree, which grew
pearly in starlight, each needle bewitched
by a spire of silk, a gift of lace. All night

the tiny spinneret flew back and forth,
fragile, anchored between inky branches;
such silent toil in small hours!

Morning came, and winter sunlight
flickered its honeyed silver against
the cottage windows, turning glittering

flimsy threads into precious skeins,
so when the widow and her children
woke, the tree was gilded, shimmering

with real silver, real gold, real joy:
despair turned into happily-ever-after,
darkness turned into light.

Olga Dermott-Bond

Ukrainian trees are often decorated with silver webs and spiders, to bring good
fortune. This tradition is inspired by a folk tale, in which a poor widow's tree
is covered in cobwebs on Christmas Eve that are transformed, by sunlight, into
silver and gold on Christmas morning.

Inheritance

Snow light through the curtains
touches the lowest branch,
where a wool angel tilts sideways,
stitched with crooked eyes,
still watching.

This tree leans,
as my father did
in his final December.
I adjust its spine with old books,
then let it lean again.

A paper dove, yellowed at the wings,
swings from threadbare string—
Aunt Miriam's, they say,
who hummed carols into heatwaves.

A gold-painted acorn
spins gently on its wire,
thumbprint hardened in glue—
my brother's, made long before
he learned how to leave things behind.

Nothing matches.
A red felt star,
its tips soft as bread edges.
A glass bell that only rings
when the wind slips through the window.

Someone once told me
grief clings to beautiful things.
Maybe that's why the tree is so full.

Every year we carry it up
from the basement—
a ritual of dust and remembering.
And every year
it stands again,
quietly holding
what we no longer can.

Molly Thapviwat